9/15/15

Miss

Let God embrace
you in His loving arms.

Mike Duff

I

THIRST

FOR

YOUR

LOVE!

Written by

Michael Seagriff

Contributor: - Dom Mark Daniel Kirby, O.S.B.

I Thirst For Your Love!

Cover and interior photographs © Michael Seagriff

Copyright © 2014 by Michael Seagriff

ISBN: SBN-13: 978-0692214657
ISBN-10: 0692214658

Printed in the United States of America

Michael Seagriff
Canastota, New York

Dedication

To our abandoned and ignored Lord,
living as a prisoner in our midst.

He who loves us even when we do not
love Him.

He Who always welcomes us back into
His healing and merciful embrace.

He   Who   thirsts   for   our   love.

Acknowledgements

I must first recognize the vital contributions Dom Mark Daniel Kirby, O.S.B., prior of the Benedictine Monks of Perpetual Adoration of the Most Holy Sacrament of the Altar, (http://cenacleosb.org and http://vultus.stblogs.org/) has made, not only to this little undertaking but to my personal understanding of and appreciation for the Eucharist and Eucharistic Adoration.

He leads "an embryonic community of monks...who intercede for the sanctification of priests" and whom God is using to reach those of His brother priests and Catholics whose fervor and love for the Eucharist has disappeared or been severely diminished.

Had Father not so generously given his permission to include *Thy Glory So Hidden and Thy Love So Despised* in Part I, *Holiness Through Adoration* in Part II, and the three articles in Part III: *Into The Shelter of My Wounded Side*, *You Pass Me By*, and *Love's Invisible Radiance*, much of this book's value would have been lost. I am grateful for his permission to include the prayers in the Appendices. In appreciation for these contributions, his community at Silverstream Priory will share in the net proceeds realized from the sale of this book.

I am also indebted to TAN Books, NC (www.tanbooks.com) for their allowing me to use the excerpts from Father Garrigou-Lagrange, O.P.'s book, *The Priest In Union With Christ*, that appear in Part IV (*Are The Masses You Attend Celebrated Worthily and Holily?*)

Table of Contents

Part III:

Part IV:

Appendices   75

(Sacred Heart Chapel, Parish of St. Vincent Ferrer, NYC)

Introduction

The time for mincing words is over.

The most significant crisis in the Catholic Church today, from which all the other problems we are experiencing flow, is the fact that an overwhelming majority of those identifying themselves as Catholic, no longer believe that our Lord Jesus Christ is really, truly and substantially present Body, Blood, Soul and Divinity in the Blessed Sacrament![1]

The sad but truthful reality is that in far too many of our Catholic parishes we have lost the sense of the sacred and an appreciation for the Holy Sacrifice of the Mass that are both essential for fostering and maintaining a belief in the Real Presence.

How can that be?

Our Church's teachings on the Eucharist are long standing, clear and include the following: the Eucharist must be the source and center of our daily lives; whenever possible Catholic Churches are to keep their doors open for some period of time each day to facilitate visits before the Blessed Sacrament; pastors are to encourage such visits; they are also to promote and encourage their parishioners' participation in Eucharistic Adoration, setting an example for their flock by doing so themselves; and they are to support the establishment and continuation of regional chapels of Perpetual Eucharistic Adoration when their own parishes are unable to sustain such a vital devotion solely by themselves.

As someone who has spent more than a dozen years coordinating Perpetual Eucharistic Adoration in a local parish and encouraging this devotion elsewhere, it has been difficult to understand at times why there is so much reluctance, if not

---

[1] Current polls, as well as what we observe with our own eyes, make it clear that an overwhelming majority, perhaps as much as 80 percent of those identifying themselves as being "Catholic", including a similar percentage of those Catholics who attend Sunday Mass, no longer believe that Jesus is really, truly and substantially present in the Sacred Eucharist.

outright opposition, to promoting Adoration - this despite our Lord's invitation for us to do so and the overwhelming evidence of the fruits that pour forth from such devotion.

The late Apostle of the Eucharist, Father John Hardon, S.J., realized "that everything, *everything*, quote EVERTHING of our faith (indeed the virtue of faith itself) depends on our faith in God being really present with us today in both His human and Divine nature, united in His Divine Person in the Holy Eucharist".

Each of us must come to that same realization if we and those around us are to be the holy people God has called us to be.

Instead of cursing this darkness, ignorance and disbelief, it's time to do something affirmative to console Our Lord and to help rediscover a sense of the "sacred" and of "awe and amazement" in this gift of the Eucharist, as Saint John Paul II and Benedict XVI had so frequently urged us to do.

We do not need any more study groups or committees or commissions in our Church. All lukewarmness toward or outright opposition to the promotion of Eucharistic Adoration and spirituality must cease. We need Bishops, priests, religious and laypeople to frequently get on their knees before their Eucharistic Lord. It is He, not any of us, Who will gift us with a deep, abiding, life-changing, sanctifying belief in His Real, Human and Divine Presence here among us. Everything else we need or think we need individually or as Church will flow from Him.

Stop a minute and ponder these Truths.

Our God does not need any of us, not even for a millisecond. Yet, as Jesus hung from the cross more than 2000 years ago, He let us know He was thirsty – not a physical thirst - but an unquenchable spiritual thirst as our Lord, Savior and Redeemer to be loved by those He created and for whose eternal benefit He died.

In the ensuing centuries, not enough of us have made sufficient effort to quench His thirst. For the most part, many of us ignore His plea to love Him as He loves us. He still thirsts for our love. He is still waiting for us to love Him! Has He not waited long enough? Why have so many of us been unwilling to quench His thirst?

There is only one credible and honest answer to that question - one that should make each of us uncomfortable but spur us to action:

If we really believed Jesus Christ was truly here with us, we would go visit Him. Nothing would prevent us from doing so. We would not permit anyone or anything to take precedence over Him. But we do not come as we ought because not enough of us believe He is here! We are the only ones who can quench His thirst. All we have to do is come into His Presence and tell Him we love Him! That's it! But most of us don't and won't.

He remains not only thirsty but heartbroken!

Shame on us for denying Him what He deserves, what He has asked of us and that which would be so very easy to give Him!

I am a simple man and can not offer a learned and theologically profound treatise on this subject. I am not qualified to do so. Moreover, such a book is not the type of writing those Our Lord longs to see, have the time or inclination to read.

Let me be frank.

Most of us spend little or no time on spiritual reading. We are one to two minute sound bite people. We do not like to read anything of any length. It is for those reasons that I kept the essays in this book brief – short sound bites intended to catch your attention and challenge you to come into His Presence or go there more frequently.

Mine is an uncomplicated approach. I invite the reader to take a reflective look at the issues raised in these short essays that I have divided into four basic themes: Lack of belief in the Real Presence; Adoration; the Priest as *alter Christus*; and the Holy Sacrifice of the Mass.

Wait a minute! If Popes, theologians, saints and brilliant lay folk have been unable to convince others to reverence, love and visit our Eucharistic God, then isn't it foolish and arrogant to think that anything a simple man may have to say on the subject will have any better results or bear any better fruit? Absolutely! It is absurd to think so. But for whatever His reason, this is the burden and passion God has placed on my heart. I must obey it.

In the end, the essays in this book are just words, observations and opinions of a simple sinful man and (thankfully) a faithful monk. But that is all we can do in response to God's never ending promptings and nudgings to share what He has placed in our hearts. Any value these words may have rests not in the men who typed and assembled them, but in He of Whom we write. We pray that by and through His power these inadequate words may penetrate, inspire and reignite the hearts of those He loves, for whose love He continues to thirst and whom He never ceases to invite into His Presence – ALL of us!

To have such a great gift, to have a God so easily accessible and not to reverence and appreciate that Gift, is the greatest of all human failings.

Love Him! Reverence Him! Visit Him! Quench His thirst!

THIS IS NO WAY

TO

TREAT GOD

IRREVERENCE

TOWARD AND LACK OF

BELIEF IN

HIS REAL PRESENCE

"Oh, if only all souls knew who is living in our Churches, there would not be so many outrages and so much disrespect in these holy places."

(St. Maria Faustina Kowalska – *Diary of Saint Faustina*)

The Elephant in Our Midst!

More than a century and half ago, St. Peter Eymard made the following observations:

"Alas, it is but too true: Our Lord in the Blessed Sacrament is not loved! He is not loved by millions of pagans, by millions of infidels, by the millions of schismatics and heretics who either do not know anything of the Eucharist or have no notions about it. Among so many thousands of creatures in whom God has placed a heart capable of loving, how many would love the Blessed Sacrament if only they knew it as I do! Must I not at least try to love it for them in their stead? Even among Catholics, few, very few love Jesus in the Most Blessed Sacrament. How many think of Him frequently, speak of Him, come to adore Him? What is the reason for this forgetfulness and coldness? People have never experienced the Eucharist, its sweetness, the delights of His Love. They have never known the goodness of Jesus! They have no idea of the extent of His love in the Most Blessed Sacrament. Some of them have faith in Jesus Christ, but a faith so lifeless and superficial that it does not reach the heart, that it contents itself with what is strictly required by conscience for their salvation. Moreover, these last are but a handful among so many other Catholics who live like moral pagans as if they had never heard of the Eucharist."

This is the greatest crisis confronting our Church today. Yet when was the last time you heard this issue addressed from the pulpit?

Which topic would you think is more deserving of being the subject of three successive weeks of preaching: the lack of belief in and reverence for the Holy Eucharist or the need to increase weekly collections?

You might be surprised at the choices some Dioceses have made in determining the relative importance of these two matters. For some, more money in the weekly collection baskets rather than an all out effort to catechize and foster reverence and belief in the Eucharistic Christ is the preferred

3

solution to the crisis of unbelief infecting Christ's Church. What a tragic choice.

We have permitted this destructive elephant of irreverence and disbelief to feel far too comfortable and welcome in our Churches. Evicting this faith destroying monster from our midst must be priority number one.

We Have Lost the Sense of the Sacred

We have lost the sense of the sacredness of Sunday. Sunday is treated no differently than any other day of the week. We have ignored Saint John Paul II's plea to reinstate the sacred nature of that day, just as we have ignored his invitation to rediscover the awe and amazement of the Eucharist. How did we get to this point? Much could be said. I offer a few observations.

We rarely mention the eternal consequences to those Catholics who choose not to attend Mass on Sunday and Holy days of obligation, and rarely if ever mention those obligations to the hundreds (if not thousands) who only attend Mass on Christmas and/or Easter. Zeal for the salvation of souls has been replaced by fear of offending someone's feelings.

Tragically, we have also lost the sense of the sacred within our Church buildings and at many of our Masses. Too many Catholics no longer believe that Jesus Christ is really, truly and substantially present in the Eucharist and in the tabernacles of our Churches. Where is the prayerful reverence and silence before and after Mass that would evidence that belief?

We ignore He Who is Love to engage in inane conversations and chatter on topics more appropriately discussed at social and sporting events. We ignore the Church's treasury of sacred music and sing instead theologically unsound songs.

We scoop the Sacred Body, Blood, Soul and Divinity of our Lord Jesus Christ out of glass dishes and gold bowls as if He were a potato chip and not the Son God. We rarely allow sufficient time to reflect on Whom we have just received and just as rarely reverently purify the Sacred vessels as we have been directed to do. Look at those around the altar. Do their actions convey a deep and abiding belief that Jesus Christ is really and truly present on the altar and in their hands?

We are not encouraged to visit the Blessed Sacrament on other days of the week and rarely (and in some parishes never) have Exposition and Benediction of the Blessed Sacrament. We lock our Church doors so those that might want to visit Him can't. Sadly, we have opened those same doors to show Al Gore's movie or to hold concerts of secular music.

If what we hear and see while at Mass or when making a visit to our Churches does not increase our awe, amazement, belief and love for the magnificent gift of the Eucharist, we are not receiving that to which we are entitled and the sacredness of Sunday will never be regained.

How Mass is celebrated and how those in the pews conduct themselves while in our Churches should not vary from parish to parish. A necessary first step toward assuring the authentic worship to which we are entitled and returning sacredness to our liturgies and our Church buildings is for all of us (ordained, religious and lay) to understand and accept what the General Instruction of the Roman Missal (GIRM) requires and to follow all of it, without exception – neither adding to nor deleting from anything prescribed therein.

Saint John Paul II made it clear that we are entitled to nothing less. Is there any valid justification for not doing so? I know of none.

Unlock The Doors Before It Is Too Late!

I was disappointed when I was not able to see You this morning. I have grown to treasure our morning visit, Mass and the reception of Your Sacred Body, Blood, Soul and Divinity- so nourishing, peaceful and transforming. I have noticed over the years that on those days I am unable or foolishly choose not to start my morning this way, the rest of my day is often more hectic and stressful. I marvel at Your great Love and Generosity in making Yourself so available to all of us. We certainly are not worthy of that love and attention.

How joyful I felt as I drove up to Your place later that same day. I did not have a great deal of time to spend with You, but You can do so much in just a few minutes. It is nice to end my day with You, however briefly our time together may be.

I began talking to You as I walked towards the Church door. As I grabbed the door handle, I was anxious to be with You. Suddenly, my peace was shattered. The door was locked. I could not get in. You were there waiting for me, but I could not get in. It was only 3:30 in the afternoon!!! Had others come and been denied admittance? So few ever visit You; how disappointed You must be when finally we come to see You but cannot get in.

This is not the first time that I have been locked out. I sometimes stop at Your other places during my travels but cannot get in. For so much of my life, I took You for granted and rarely thought of You. Now I am incensed when we are kept apart. You told St. Margaret Mary Alacoque that you have a "terrible thirst to be loved by your creatures in the Most Blessed Sacrament". You gave us this gift of Yourself. You long for us to visit and to show You heartfelt appreciation for all that You have done for us.

I want to spend time in Your presence. I want my visits to be acts of reparation for all the offenses against Your Sacred Heart, including those that I have committed. I know that You are with me wherever I am. But You are really, substantially and most especially present in the tabernacles of all the Catholic Churches throughout the world, even if, in some of these structures, Your tabernacle is hidden. Like little Francisco of Fatima, I want to spend some time with my "hidden Jesus". You are the only thing of everlasting value in these buildings.

Why (as St. Peter Julian Eymard observed more than 100 years ago) do we have time for everything except for visits to our Lord and God, Who is waiting and longing for us in the Blessed Sacrament? Why do so few visit You? Why are those who try to do so often locked out? Why are Your Church and its members so timid and so silent about this great mystery and gift? Why have we lost reverence for and belief in Your Real Presence?

Why do our activities in Church before Mass more resemble a social hour than silent preparation for the reception of Your Body, Blood, Soul and Divinity? How can we show You reverence when we sometimes have no kneelers? Why is there so often no silent time for us to thank You after receiving this magnificent gift? How can we adequately thank You over the music and singing? How can we demonstrate our reverence and appreciation for this Gift if sometimes we no sooner get to our pew then Mass continues?

Perhaps if silence were to return to our Churches before Mass, following the Eucharist and after Mass ended, reverence for You would be restored. Perhaps if the use of extraordinary ministers of the Eucharist was not so ordinary and if we saw all of your priests and people handle and receive Your Body and Blood more reverently, we would have a greater appreciation for Your Real Presence. Perhaps if we were reminded each Sunday at Mass by words and by what we see that You are really and substantially present in the tabernacle, more of us would come. Perhaps if we were encouraged to visit You, more would do so.

Perhaps if we knew that "every moment we spend in the presence of the Blessed Sacrament deepens our union with Jesus, transforms us into the very image and likeness of God Himself, and makes up for those who do not know Him or do not love Him", more would come.

Perhaps if we knew that our late Holy Father (Saint John Paul II) had asked that there be Perpetual Adoration in every Catholic Church throughout the world, more of us would come. Perhaps if we were taught that "every holy hour draws the world and everyone in it closer to Christ", more would come. Perhaps if we knew that "every holy hour lifts up the whole world to the Father for His blessing", more would come. Perhaps if we knew that "every holy hour would save a soul from going to hell and bring that soul to heaven", more of us would come.

Why do we fail to "adore and visit Jesus, abandoned and forsaken in His Sacrament of Love"? Is not the time long past due for all in Your Church to teach more clearly and more emphatically of Your Real Presence and the need for us to spend time in That transforming Presence? Is not our wholehearted response to John Paul II's plea (echoed repeatedly by his successor Pope Benedict XVI) that we rediscover "a sense of awe and amazement in the Eucharist", also long overdue?

When I initially wrote this reflection several years ago, I humbly suggested that the Catholic Church respond to this sad reality by first unlocking the doors of its Churches and by reinstating "silence" as the reverent language spoken there. Small but essential steps, I thought. "Jesus will be pleased," I wrote then. "He will transform our families, our Church, our communities and us."

Unfortunately, not enough parishes have implemented these simple steps. Is there any wonder that rampant disbelief in Your Real Presence continues, or that so many of our "locked Churches" have since been "permanently closed" and our Lord evicted?

Where Have They Taken Him?

When I travel and enter unfamiliar Catholic Churches, I don't really ask for much: an atmosphere of reverent silence and a tabernacle in front of which I may momentarily kneel and worship my Eucharistic Lord.

One would expect our Lord to be in "a distinguished place ... conspicuous, suitably adorned and conducive to prayer". But often His whereabouts are unknown. Far too often, instead of kneeling before the King of Kings and Lord of Lords, I have to assemble a search team to scour the Church building to find out where they have taken Him! This should never be! But it occurs far too frequently.

My daughter and her family recently moved to a new town in a new State. We went to visit them. We also went to visit our Lord in the two Catholic Churches located in this town. He was no where to be seen! After searching for Him in the larger of the two Churches, I found Him in a chapel set apart from the area where the congregation gathers and celebrates Mass. I never did find where they had taken Him in the other Church!

A few days before this upsetting experience, I was blessed to attend the annual conference of the Catholic Marketing Network and the Catholic Writers' Guild. These groups had no difficulty placing a tabernacle prominently behind the altar that had been set up in one of the hotel's banquet rooms.

They also had no problem processing with our Eucharistic Lord from the hallways of one hotel to repose the Sacred Monstrance in an Adoration Chapel set up in an adjoining hotel. This all took place in a secular setting with hundreds of committed Catholics unabashedly and publicly singing "Holy God, We Praise They Name".

Our Church buildings must be sacred places in which the tabernacle where Our Lord resides is prominently and conspicuously placed and readily visible to everyone upon entry. No one should ever have to search for Him after entering His Church.

How blessed I was to give witness to my belief in His Eucharistic Presence by processing with Him through the halls of two secular buildings. How tragic that I could not readily find Him in two of His Churches.

It's Enough To Make God And A Grown Man Cry

What if you had given everything you had (including your life) in order that others might live but only a handful of those for whom you died seemed to care? What if you returned ready to comfort, strengthen and sustain them through life's daily challenges and struggles, but only a small number acknowledged your presence among them and even fewer spent time with you or sought your aid? What if the majority of people totally ignored you and acted as if you were not even there?

If you or I were treated this way, we would cry. Jesus, the King of King and Lords of Lords, is treated that way day after day by many who claim to be Catholic. Yet, so great is His love for us that He chooses to remain locked in the tabernacles of His churches, every day, waiting for us to acknowledge His presence among us, to visit and speak to Him, and to ask for His help.

He too must have recently cried. I'll tell you why.

A man entered a Catholic church a few days ago to spend some quiet time in the soothing loving presence of His Lord. He was the only one there. He kneeled and prayerfully pleaded with Him to protect and heal his granddaughter and return peace to her young but troubled heart. The silence, solitude and flickering candles brought peace to his heart as this man gazed upon his imprisoned Lord.

This consoling silence was short-lived, however, as one parent after another arrived to pick up their elementary school age children from religious education class. It was not too long before this quiet and sacred place was filled with the din of loud adult voices discussing the burning issues of parenthood, politics and current economic challenges - no matter that their Lord was just a few feet in front of them; no matter the presence of a man obviously attempting to pray.

13

This man saw no visible evidence in the actions of these adults that any of them really believed that Jesus Christ was really, truly and substantially present, Body, Blood, Soul and Divinity in the Sacred Eucharist reserved in the Church's tabernacle or that any of them even thought this would be an appropriate time for them to silently pray. As their children began to filter into the Church from the parish hall, bedlam followed them and the last vestiges of sacredness vanished, save for the one sole man sitting and silently praying, determined to offer good example. Maybe he should have spoken to these parents and their children. How will they learn if no one teaches or corrects them? No one did.

The conduct this man observed must not occur in the presence of such a loving God. It happened not only that afternoon but happens every Sunday (if not more often) in far too many of our Catholic parishes. These disrespectful behaviors will continue to occur so long as a majority of Catholics no longer believe that Christ is really, truly and substantially present in the Eucharist.

Catholic Churches are intended to be sacred places – different from all other structures in which we spend time – a silent prayerful oasis of quiet, comfort, solace and grace. The stark reality that we have lost that sense and our belief in the Real Presence, is enough to make Our Lord cry.

We must insist on reverent silence in our Churches. Hard to believe but we must re-teach this fundamental truth. Our every action while within our Church buildings must evidence our belief that we are in a sacred place and in the presence of God – otherwise the rest of what we teach or do in Church will be for naught.

It would be so easy to correct this tragic situation if more of our priests would remind us at Sunday Mass as to the proper way to conduct ourselves while in this sacred place and the reasons for doing so. Their instruction and example can be lovingly reinforced by conspicuously posting a reminder at all entrances that "Silence is the reverent language spoken here".

So why do more of our priests not do so? Their continued failure to teach us makes this grown man cry.

Why? Where? - Some Challenging Thoughts on the Eucharist

Why Lord do I not leap for joy whenever I am in Your Presence as St. John the Baptist did while in the womb of his mother Elizabeth?

Why do I take Your Presence in the Eucharist for granted?

Where is the awe and amazement that should overcome me whenever You are placed on my tongue?

Where are the tears of joy and gratitude that should freely flow from the eyes of such an unworthy recipient of Love Himself as You penetrate and saturate every cell of this earthen vessel with Your Sacred Blood?

Why do I ever allow myself to be distracted by anyone or anything else during these intimate moments with You?

Why do I sometimes unconsciously thwart and impede the graces You intend to shower upon me as You and I are physically united?

Why am I so often in a rush to leave Church and abruptly end our intimate visit?

Why Lord do I fail to love You and Your Blessed Mother as much as You and she love me?

Why?

Oh, Father You Must Not Be Aware of What You Are Doing!

I was on the road recently and stopped at a nearby parish for daily Mass.

As Father elevated the Sacred Host, I intended to gaze upon the Body, Blood, Soul and Divinity of my loving Lord Jesus Christ, and to silently utter the prayer of adoration first offered by a doubting St. Thomas, "My Lord and my God".

Before I was able to lip the word "My", our Lord was no longer visible. Father flicked his wrist and like a Frisbee threw our Lord unceremoniously on to His golden paten throne.

Oh, Father, you must not be aware of what you are doing!

Surely, if you saw what I saw, Father, you would no longer act that way.

Oh, how our Lord deserves to be held aloft long enough for all of us present to reverently adore Him. Certainly, He deserves to then be placed reverently and ever so carefully upon the paten.

Oh, Father, you must not be aware of what you are doing!

Let us pray daily for all of our priests.

Pray specifically, as St. Peter Julian Eymard recommends in his *Litany of the Most Blessed Sacrament*, "that all priests have a profound love of the Holy Eucharist" and that "they celebrate the Holy Sacrifice of the Mass in accordance with its sublime dignity."

And consider having the courage to frame the following prayer (which is actually posted on a wall leading to a chapel of the Sisters of Charity in Rome, Italy) and asking your pastor to display it in the sacristy where he vests:

17

"Oh, priest, celebrate this Mass as if it were your first Mass.
Oh, priest, celebrate this Mass as if were your only Mass.
Oh, priest, celebrate this Mass as if it were your last Mass."

Thy Glory So Hidden, and Thy Love So Despised

[A prayer of adoration and reparation pronounced aloud before the Most Holy Sacrament following Vespers.]

Lord Jesus Christ,

God from God, Light from Light, true God from true God begotten of the Father before the daystar, and consubstantial Virgin Mary, by the power of the Holy Spirit, I adore Thee, who art truly present here, and, out of my own poverty and weakness, I desire to make reparation for those who do not adore Thee in this wondrous Sacrament, and for those who deny the mystery of Thy real presence.

I would make reparation as well for those who approach Thee without reverence, for those who touch, and handle, and receive Thy adorable Body with coldness, with indifference, and with little awareness of the immensity of Thy charity burning in this Most Holy Sacrament.

Thou art here upon the altar just as Thou wert in the cave of Bethlehem, where, wrapped in swaddling bands, Thou wast laid in the manger as upon an altar, the innocent Lamb made ready for the sacrifice, the Living Bread come down from heaven, and set forth upon the altars of Thy Church for the nourishment of those whom Thou hast created to partake of Thy Flesh and Blood and, in so doing, to become one with Thee. Here, though Thy glory be veiled, yet is it visible, for one cannot gaze upon the Sacred Host without reflecting, as in a mirror, something of the radiance of Thy glory hidden beneath Its humble appearance.

I unite my adoration first to that of the Virgin Mother and of Saint Joseph, desiring, in some way, to adore Thee with them and to abide in their company. I adore Thee in communion with the Angelic Choirs who filled the skies of Bethlehem on that most holy night, and I adore Thee together with the lowly shepherds who, crossing over to Bethlehem, found there that everything was just as the Angel told them.

Receive my adoration here, and in every church become the true House of Bread, by reason of Thine adorable presence, thus prolonging the mystery of Bethlehem through space and through time, from the rising of the sun to its setting.

Bowing low before Thee, I adore and I submit to this mystery of Thy omnipotence become so fragile, of Thy glory so hidden, and of Thy love so despised. Let all that is in me surrender in faith to what I see before my eyes, and to what I do not see, for Thou art here, who livest and reignest with the Father, in the unity of the Holy Spirit, one God, forever and ever. Amen.

(An Act of Honorable Amendment –A Mectildian-Benedictine practice)

Adoration

Our Abandoned

And

Forgotten

Privilege

"I thirst for you. Yes, that is the only way to even begin to describe my love for you: I thirst for you. And to be loved by you – That is how precious you are to Me."

(Meditation *"I Thirst"* used by Missionaries of Charity)

A Reflection On Unrequited Love

We can not get to know another person or develop a loving relationship with that individual unless we spend time with him or her. To say that you love someone, but never visit, engage in conversation with or spend time with that individual would be to live a lie and deceive yourself.

God is calling each of us to a personal and intimate encounter and relationship with Him. But how can we experience such a relationship if we do not get to know Him, or spend time with Him, or talk to Him, or lay our burdens before Him, or listen to Him, or trust Him? Just as we could not maintain our physical health by limiting physical nourishment to one hour a week, we are foolish to think that our mere presence in a Church building on Sunday for an hour can create and sustain the type of intimate spiritual relationship God offers and desires with each of us.

Oh, how He Who is love is not loved in return! He hungers to have you acknowledge His Real Presence in the Eucharist.

He desires to fill you with His peace, comfort and love. He wants you to come and lay your burdens down before Him. He wishes to strengthen you in your daily duties, trials and challenges. He longs to make you like Him and to equip and sustain you as you become more Christ-like to others. But God will not force Himself on anyone. Each of us must freely respond to His invitation.

So let me ask you: Where does God rate in your life? How much do you love Him and how important is He to you in your daily and weekly lives? How much time each week do you think of Him and devote to Him in contrast to the time you spend caring for yourself and family, working, eating, watching television, using the computer, gambling, sleeping, engaging in sports, socializing with friends and families, participating in community programs?

Look at the 24 hours in each day and the 168 hours in each week and see how often you have anything to do with Him. For most of us, I would imagine the answer is not much.

In many Dioceses of this country, we Catholics are blessed to have Churches in which someone is always present with Our Lord, praying 24 hours a day, seven days a week, 365 days a year. Remarkable isn't it? - a life-changing experience for those who (often at great personal sacrifice) spend one specific hour each week in the presence of our Eucharistic Lord; a devotion most pleasing to Him Who is deserving of our worship, adoration and praise; and the source of untold blessings to so many in our families and communities.

God has blessed our Churches with His Real Presence where He can be worshiped, adored and loved, where He changes, heals and comforts the hearts and souls (and sometimes bodies) of many. Yet few come to keep Him company or to make reparation to Him for those who do not believe in Him. Where are the courageous prayer warriors willing to get up in the early morning hours to be with Him while the rest of us sleep? How sad and lonely is Our Lord – so intimately present among us but ignored by the majority of people claiming to love Him.

Jesus asked his disciples in Gethsemane, and He is asking each of us right now: "Could you not watch one hour with Me?" What an affront, insult and gesture of ingratitude it would be to such a caring, loving and merciful God if (where it exists) Perpetual Eucharistic Adoration devotions had to be curtailed because so few of His people loved Him enough to be with Him.

Belief in the Real Presence of our Lord in the Blessed Sacrament is a gift from God. No one but He can give it to you. He will do just that if you trust Him enough to spend time with Him. He awaits you with open and loving arms. If you come to Him with an open heart, He will give you His! That's His promise!

What are you waiting for? Consider this a personal invitation from the King of Kings and Lord of Lords! He will transform you, your family and the communities in which you worship, live and work.

Why Don't We?

The Jewish people knew when Moses entered the Tent and a column of cloud stood at the entrance of that Tent that God was there with him. The burning tabernacle candle, not a column of cloud, signifies our Lord's Presence among us today.

The Jews knew the Tent was a sacred, holy place and acted accordingly. Unable to enter it themselves, they stood at the entrances of their own tents and worshipped their Lord. How we must rediscover that sense of the sacred and holy within our Church buildings. Our Lord is as much present there as He was in the Tent with Moses. He beckons us to enter.

God spoke to Moses face to face as one man would speak to another. Let us appreciate that we can sit with our faces turned to our imprisoned Lord in the tabernacles of His Churches and converse with Him. Even better yet, let us run to gaze upon His Humble Presence, whenever He is exposed in the Sacred Monstrance.

Just as He gave Moses the Ten Commandments to share with his people, so too He will instruct us if we would but spend time with Him and adore Him Who is really and substantially present in the Blessed Sacrament.

No one loves us more than our God. He Who is Love waits just for us. How blessed we are to be able to come into His Presence. Why don't we?

Enter Into His Presence

Luke's Gospel (Luke 1:5-25) prompts these simple thoughts:

The Jewish people were so filled with awe, amazement, respect and reverent fear for the Ark of the Covenant located in their midst, that only once a year was the high priest permitted to enter the inner sanctuary of the tabernacle and go behind the veil that separated the "Holy of Holies" from the "Holy Place", the Temple's second holiest chamber, and the rest of the temple area. The other Jewish priests burned incense and offered prayers in the "Holy Place" at the morning and evening sacrifices while crowds prayed in the Temple courts.[2] Priests like Zechariah drew lots to determine which one of their priestly number would be selected to enter and incense this sacred space. It was a great honor and privilege for the priest chosen to experience this intimate encounter with the Lord – something the average Jew could never experience.

Today, we Catholics can approach the tabernacles in our Churches where our Lord is really, truly and substantially present in the Blessed Sacrament anytime we enter those sacred buildings. We do not have to draw straws. We do not have to be ordained priests. We do not have to limit our visit to just once a year. We can be with Him every single day. The choice is up to us. Yet, far too few of us ever make that choice. Consequently, our God, the Prince of Peace, often remains alone, abandoned, and forgotten.

Is there any wonder why chaos rather than peace reigns in so many hearts, in our Church and throughout the world?

Go visit He Who Is and let Him change your heart!

---

[2] From *Ignatius Catholic Study Bible New Testament*

Our Lord Deserves It!

Adoration is not for a handful or a selected few. It is for everyone. It is what our loving Lord asks for, and more importantly, what He deserves.

Saint John Paul II went so far as to urge EVERY parish in the world to have Perpetual Eucharistic Adoration.

Let me put one hour of Adoration each week into proper perspective for you by borrowing and adapting a few interesting statistics offered by Father Oscar Lukefahr, CM.[3]

If you live to be eighty, you would have spent about three years reading, five years talking, six years riding in a car, seven years eating, eleven years in recreational activities and twenty-seven years sleeping. If you offered an hour of Adoration each week, you would have given our Lord less than six months of your time. Add attendance at Sunday Mass for an hour every week and praying for five minutes every day to your weekly hour of Adoration, we are still talking of offering Him less than one year of your life.

"How can we refuse so little to a loving God," asks Father Lukefahr, "who has given us so much?" May I ask the same question?

Sadly, there are some Catholics, not few in number, who have neither seen a monstrance nor attended Benediction and Exposition of the Blessed Sacrament. How is that possible?

According to Father Martin Lucia, a Missionary of the Blessed Sacrament, more Catholics would likely come to adore the King of Kings and Lord of Lords, if they knew that: every moment they spend in the presence of the Blessed Sacrament would deepen their union with Christ; transform them into the very image and likeness of God Himself; make

---

[3] "We Worship – A Guide to the Catholic Mass" page 17)

up for those who do not know Him or who do not love Him; and bring about the radical transformation of the whole world. If Catholics also knew that when they go before the Lord in the Blessed Sacrament they stand in the place of the one person in the world who does not know God or who is the furthest away from God, or the most in need of His mercy, that they bring upon that soul – they win for that soul – the grace of salvation to turn back to God, to go to heaven instead of hell, and that they gain for that person the grace of salvation – our Lord would never be left alone.

Belief in the Real Presence is an act of faith and a gift from our Lord. That being said, if a pastor does all that he can to teach the truths set forth above, to restore and maintain a sense of the sacred within the confines of his Church building, if he properly and regularly catechizes his flock, if his every action evidences his deep seeded belief, sense of awe, amazement in and dependence on the Blessed Sacrament, and if he participates in, promotes and treasures Adoration himself, his parishioners will come to do likewise.

"If you build it, they will come" was a punch line in a movie a few years back.

Jesus invites his imperfect creatures to come into His Presence so He can make them more like Himself. Most able bodied persons can find one hour each week to be with their Lord and Savior (even if it is in 10 or 15 minute segments). Many simply choose not to do so. Others find only locked Churches.

When You Next Come Into His Presence

What is your response when you first come into the Presence of Your Lord?

Do you adore Him by genuflecting before the tabernacle where He has been eagerly awaiting your arrival? When you get to the pew do you kneel down and talk to Him or do you spend the time before Mass catching up with your neighbors?

What should your response be?

There are valuable lessons to learn from Elizabeth's reaction (and that of the child in her womb) to Mary's visitation.

"Who am I," the pregnant octogenarian asked as John the Baptist leaped for joy, "that the mother of my Lord should come to me?" Mary was the first tabernacle. Clearly, Elizabeth and her son recognized in whose Presence they were.

When was the last time you leaped for joy (spiritually or physically) as you approached the tabernacle, or gazed upon Our Lord exposed in a Monstrance or when He was placed on your tongue?

When you approach the sanctuary to receive the Body, Blood, Soul and Divinity of your Lord and Savior does He see an appreciative and joyful face or a distracted and joyless one? If it is the latter, ask Him for a new heart so overflowing with love for Him that such love will be reflected on your face.

Has God ever heard you ask Him in the stillness of your soul and the quiet of your heart right before you receive Him: "Who am I that my Lord should come to me?" If not, return to your pew and quietly ponder that question and the miracle you experience every time you receive Communion at Mass.

How will you respond the next time you're in His Presence?

Thank You For Coming!

When I entered this world, my Blessed Mother and her most chaste spouse, Joseph, welcomed Me with loving arms, eyes and hearts. A choir of heavenly angels surrounded and serenaded us!

My heart leaped for joy when the humble shepherds came and paid Me homage. I smiled! We waited.

But none of the religious, political or social leaders bothered to visit. They never thought to look for Me. I cried! Even today, centuries after my arrival, most of them rarely think of Me. I cry!

Then the foreign dignitaries came. They had left their country in search of the Truth, not knowing on their departure, exactly Where, What or Who that Truth was but certain they would find It. They did - the Incarnate Truth wrapped in swaddling clothes and lying in a manger - and they were forever changed. I smiled!

My parents and I had to flee to Egypt to thwart Herod's plan to murder Me. He killed other Innocents instead. Oh, how we cried! This type of evil continues to manifest itself today. We still cry!

As I embarked on my public ministry, many welcomed my miracles but later rejected Me. Only My Mother, Mary Magdalene, My Beloved disciple John and a handful of women walked the *Via Dolorosa* with me and watched them nail me to the cross. They cried.

I rose from the dead in order to restore eternal life to those who would believe in Me - so many still do not. I cry!

I remain physically here among those I love - Body, Blood, Soul and Divinity - in the Most Blessed Sacrament, waiting for them to visit. Few ever come. Hardly anyone believes I am really and substantially present here among them. I cry!

So you can imagine the ineffable joy I experienced when this Chapel of Perpetual Eucharistic Adoration opened and each of you, one by one, sometimes in pairs, began visiting me for an hour each week. You still come these many years later, often at great sacrifice, even when you are tired, discouraged, overwhelmed with worry, anxiety, illness or distraught over the death of a loved one.

You have given Me the greatest gift possible – yourself, your time, and your heart. Your presence here with Me is a source of great comfort and a most welcomed act of reparation for the general indifference so many display toward my Pierced and Sacred Heart!

When you next visit and see Me encased in this modest Monstrance blessed by my beloved John Paul II and so majestically held up by this angelic throne, know that I look at you lovingly as tears of joy flow from my Sacred Face in appreciation for the gift of your presence.

I love you more than you are able to presently understand. I desire to hold you eternally in My arms! Will you let Me?

Holiness Through Adoration

The practice of adoration is not difficult. It is a gentle abiding in My Presence, a resting in the radiance of My Eucharistic Face, a closeness to My Eucharistic Heart.

Words, though sometimes helpful, are not necessary, nor are thoughts. What I seek from one who would adore Me in spirit and in truth is a heart aflame with love, a heart content to abide in My Presence, silent and still, engaged only in the act of loving Me and of receiving My love. Though this is not difficult, it is, all the same, my own gift to the soul who asks for it. Ask, then, for the gift of adoration.

Adoration is an austere prayer because it rests upon faith alone. Out of faith there rises the pure flame of hope, and out of the flame of hope, I enkindle in the soul a great conflagration of charity; that is, a communication to the soul of the fire that blazes in My Eucharistic Heart.

The fire of Divine Love does not destroy what I created: a soul fashioned in My image and likeness. It purifies that soul and burns away only what is incompatible with My infinite holiness, and with the purity of My Essence. The soul, however, is not annihilated. The soul remains, even in the midst of the purifying flames of Divine Love, fully capable of believing, of hoping, and of loving Me.

Adoration is a furnace and a forge. The soul called to a life of adoration must expect to suffer the intensity of the fiery furnace, and the reshaping of all that is misshapen in her in the forge of My Divine Will. For this to happen, it is enough that the soul offers Herself to My love and remain humble, peaceful, and quiet as I purify and transform My Presence.

If only souls knew the power to purify and to transform that emanates from My tabernacles! If only My priests knew this they would hasten into My presence and remain there, waiting for Me to do in them what, of themselves, they cannot do. It is the simple prayer of adoration that renders a priest fit for the sacred ministry by giving him a pure heart and by correcting all that is incompatible with My Divine Holiness and with My Priestly Love in his life. This way of holiness through adoration is a secret revealed to My saints in ages past, and it is a gift that I am offering My priests in these times of impurity, persecution, and darkness.

For impurity, I will give them a shining purity that will blaze before the eyes of the world as a testimony to Divine Love. For persecution I will give them a manly strength and resoluteness of purpose that will confound those who plot their downfall. For darkness I will give them a clear light by which to order their steps and see what choices are pleasing to My Heart.

Time spent in My presence is not time wasted. It is the ground and support of every word spoken by My priests in the exercise of their ministry; it is the secret of a priestly action that is supernaturally fruitful, bearing fruit that will last.

If this is true of the priests whom I have chosen to labor in the vineyard of My Church, how much more must it be true of [those] whom I have chosen and set apart to live cloistered in the Cenacle with My Most Holy Mother and with Saint John, My Beloved Disciple.

John was most at home in My Eucharistic presence and in the company of My Mother. John understood better and more than the other Apostles the mysteries that I instituted in the Cenacle on the night before I suffered. John was the first of a long line of Eucharistic priests called to love Me and abide in My Eucharistic presence, close to My Heart, and in the radiance of My Face.

This is the particular grace that Saint John would share with those who, responding to My call, will find their way to the Cenacle of adoration that I am bringing to birth as a living organism within My Church, enlivened by the Holy Spirit and formed in the Heart of My Immaculate Mother.

(From *In Sinu Iesu*, The Journal of a Priest)

The Priest

The *Altus Christus*

Among Us

Love Them

Pray For Them

Support Them

Challenge Them

"To live in the midst of the world without wishing its pleasures; to be a member of each family, yet belonging to none; to share all sufferings, to penetrate all secrets; to heal all wounds; to go from men to God and offer Him their prayers; to return from God to men bring pardon and hope; to have a heart of fire for charity and a heart of bronze for chastity; to teach and to pardon, console and bless always —what a glorious life! And it is yours, O Priest of Jesus Christ!"

(Father Jean Baptiste Henri-Dominque Lacordaire, O.P.)

Our Priests

According to St. Pius X, our sanctity depends in large measure on the holiness of our priests. Every day and most especially each Holy Thursday is an appropriate time to reflect on our priests, the imperative that the Eucharist be the source, center and summit of their and our lives, and our duty as laity to treasure, encourage and support them.

We begin by recalling how eloquently St. Gregory of Nazianzus, Doctor of our Church, wrote of what it is to be a priest:

> *"We must begin by purifying ourselves before purifying others; we must be instructed to be able to instruct, become light to illuminate, draw close to God to bring Him close to others, be sanctified to sanctify, lead by the hand and counsel prudently...I know God's greatness and man's weakness but also his potential. The priest is the defender of Truth, who stands with angels, gives glory with archangels, causes sacrifices to rise to the altar on high, shares Christ's priesthood, refashions creation, restores it in God's image, recreates it for the world on high and, even greater, is divinized and divinizes."*

In 1962 Venerable Fulton Sheen advised his fellow priests that they "become significant to their fellow men not by being 'a regular guy' but by being 'another Christ'." He foresaw the failings of his brother priests, as "a want of lively faith in the Divine Presence". He was just as astute to recognize that "the sanctity of the priesthood starts there too". He warned prophetically that "every worldly priest hinders the growth of the Church; every saintly priest promotes it". He prayed that God would make each of His priests "*alter Christus*". That too should be our prayer.

The perspectives of St. Gregory and St. Pius X and the observations of Archbishop Sheen remain as valid and

39

essential for us and our priests today as when they first shared them. Zeal for the salvation of souls cannot be replaced with a misguided emphasis on community organizing and social justice issues. The Fathers of Vatican Council II made this clear when they wrote in *Gaudium et Spes* that "Christ did not bequeath to the Church a mission in the political, economic or social order: the purpose he assigned to it was a religious one". The physical well-being of people (a notable goal and obligation for all) must of necessity be secondary to their eternal salvation.

No one expresses this vital truth more clearly than St. John Chrysostom:

> *"Zeal for the salvation of souls is of so great a merit before God, that to give up all our goods to the poor, or to spend our whole life in the exercises of all sorts of austerities cannot equal the merit of it. There is no service more agreeable to God than this one. To employ one's life in this blessed labor is more pleasing to the Divine Majesty than to suffer martyrdom. Would you not feel happy if you could spend large sums of money in corporal works of mercy? But know that he who labors for the salvation of souls does far more; nay, the zeal of souls is of far greater merit before God...than the working of miracles."*

Our priests are under enormous pastoral and administrative burdens and are, have been and will continue to be viciously and relentlessly subjected to spiritual attack by the Evil One who knows full well that without priests there will be no Eucharist. We can not allow that to happen.

They, like each of us, are human and prone to sin. Sadly, some of our priests have grievously sinned and exposed a foul stench within their midst. Fortunately, the majority of our priests have not succumbed to such filth. But our priests can faithfully fulfill their role as "another Christ" only with the grace of God – abundant grace flowing to all priests for whom the Eucharist is the source, center and summit of their priestly lives, who treasure offering the Holy Sacrifice of the Mass daily, who spend time before the Blessed Sacrament each day, and who have developed a deep and trusting relationship with and devotion to our Blessed Mother.

They need our prayers, our support and encouragement. Never a day should pass by without each of us getting on our knees, thanking God for the faithful priests he has sent and will be sending to help us on our path to personal sanctification and eternal salvation and asking Him to provide them with all they need to be faithful to their vocation and successful against the attacks of the Evil One. Regularly lift these heroic men up in prayer before the Blessed Sacrament, fast on their behalf, offer a daily rosary for their sanctification, regularly go to confession to them, and let them know that you appreciate them even when the Truth they share may cause you to take a closer look at yourself, your relationship with God and your fidelity to the teachings of His Church.

If we do all that, in God's perfect timing, each of us will be able to say about all our priests, the same thing one lawyer reportedly said when, after returning from seeing St. John Vianney in Ars, someone asked him what he had seen there: "I saw God in a man."

St. John Vianney, Holy Priests and Zeal For Salvation of Souls

The feast day for St. John Marie Vianney should garner more attention than it does or will. What a shame!

Despite the pleas of Saint John Paul II and Benedict XVI that their priests follow this holy man's example, this patron saint of priests is too often ignored. How can that be?

It is clear from a cursory review of his writings that the Cure's primary concern was for the sanctification and salvation of the souls entrusted to him. Here is a sampling of what he had to say:

> "Lord, make my people holy. This is one thing I ask of you. And if they are not holy, I know it will be my fault. But make them holy."

> "My God, grant me the conversion of my parish, and I am willing to suffer all my life whatsoever it may please You to lay upon me; yes, even for a hundred years am I prepared to endure the sharpest pains, only let my people be converted."

> "I can't stop praying for poor sinners who are on the road to hell. If they come to die in that state, they will be lost for all eternity. What a pity! We have to pray for sinners! Praying for sinners is the most beautiful and useful of prayers because the just are on the way to heaven, the souls of purgatory are sure to enter there, but the poor sinners will be lost forever. All devotions are good but there is no better one than such prayer for sinners."

I Thirst For Your Love

"There is nothing, so great as the Eucharist. If God had something more precious, He would have given it to us."

"We ought to visit him [Jesus in the Holy Eucharist] often. How dear to Him is a quarter of an hour spared from our occupations or from some useless employment, to come and pray to Him, visit Him, and console Him for all the ingratitude He receives! When He sees poor souls hurrying to Him, He smiles at them. They come with that simplicity which pleases Him so much, to ask pardon for all sinners, and for the insults of so many who are ungrateful."

"Were we to fully realize what a priest is on earth, we would die: not of fright but of love...Without the priest, the passion and death of our Lord would be of no avail. It is the priest who continues the work of redemption on earth...What use would be a house filled with gold, were there no one to open its door? The priest holds the key to the treasures of heaven: it is he who opens the door; he is the steward of the good Lord; the administrator of His goods."

Today then is a time to be bold. So I must ask: Should any of our present priests have any less concern for their sanctification and salvation and that of their flock than this humble, holy priest had for his? Not surprisingly, the Cure left an unambiguous answer:

"Woe to the pastor, who remains silent, while God is offended and souls are lost."

43

Community organizing, political activism, and social justice programs will not save souls. Only God working through holy priests will.

Love Your Priests – All Of Them

Saint John Paul II gave the Church many beautiful gifts; among them were the Year of the Rosary (2002-2003) and the Year of the Eucharist (2004-2005). In doing so, he encouraged priests, religious and laity to use these gifts and harness the spiritual power and strength that flows from them. Both he and his successor have urged their priests to make the Eucharist the source, center and summit of their priestly lives and to fully embrace and live their unique vocation as "another Christ."

During the Year for the Priest (2009-2010) Pope Emeritus Benedict XVI held St. John Marie Vianney up as the model for all priests because the Cure of Ars accepted the cross, was full of zeal for the salvation of souls, was an ardent Adorer of the Blessed Sacrament, was greatly devoted to our Blessed Mother, a lover of sinners who spent hours daily reconciling them with their merciful God, a model of purity, humble in all things, lover of penance and mortification, and a good and holy priest.

Not a single priest should be hesitant to imitate this great priest and saint! There have always been John Vianneys in our midst. Thankfully, more priests are responding positively and wholeheartedly to the Holy Father's challenge. We are beginning to experience the fruits of their faithful embrace of that call! While we certainly need more priests, we first need holy priests whose Christ-like example will attract other men to the priesthood they love.

Unfortunately, some have rejected this humble and obedient man as a model for their priestly lives. This should not be surprising. We know from the words of the prophet Malachi and sadly from our own contemporary experiences that there will always be some who "have turned aside from the way and have caused many to falter by their instruction" (Malachi 2:8).

There are a multitude of reasons why some priests have chosen not to follow the Cure's example. There are those who have succumbed to a false sense of humility believing they are not capable of living such a life; or who refuse to make the Eucharist the source, center and summit of their priestly lives; or who have abandoned the cross, the altar, the pulpit, fraternal correction, the confessional, zeal for the salvation of souls or a life of self-sacrifice; or who have treated their priesthood as if it were no different than the secular vocations of lay men and women, by becoming community organizers and social activists instead of fishers of men; or who have placed a premium on being politically correct; or who have devoted most of their energies to the worldly sphere of influence instead of the supernatural and eternal one that flows from the Eucharist and the confessional; or who have failed to faithfully teach and defend the Truths of our Faith; or who, instead of "faithful assent" to all of the Church's teachings, mislead themselves and untold numbers of others by suggesting that there is such a thing as "faithful dissent"; or who have remained silent in the presence of sin; or who have abandoned clerical dress for worldly attire; or who aspire to be treated more as a "regular guy" than "another Christ"; or who prefer to be called "sacramental minster" rather than a priest.

Our priests have supernatural tasks which cannot be done by relying on their natural abilities. Yet some insist on trying to. How sad it is whenever I hear one of Christ's overburdened priests claim that there are days when they are so busy they don't pray! How can that be? Did not Jesus tell Martha to set her priorities in the right order? Were not the Cure of Ars, Fulton Sheen, Saint John Paul II and Blessed Mother Teresa busy people? Yet each of them spent at least one hour daily in front of the Blessed Sacrament because they knew it was He not them who would accomplish that which He asked them to do. Never once did their daily Holy Hour impede their ability to complete God's work. To the contrary, it was because of their daily faithfulness to spending time in His

Presence that they were able to do what they did. Why do so many doubt this truth?

Where are the lay people who have the expertise to do the worldly tasks that drain so much time and energy out of men who were ordained first and foremost for the salvation of souls, to say Mass, to forgive sins and to administer the other Sacraments? None of our priests should be bookkeepers, financiers, purchasers, social workers, community organizers or clerks of the works. They are and must be about saving souls! Similarly, we lay people should be about using our skills to lighten our priests' administrative tasks and evangelizing the unique areas in which we live and work instead of yearning for quasi-clerical positions.

The good news is that despite any shortcomings among some of our priests, all of them can yet be the holy priests God called them to be and that we need. They must put the Eucharist and the Mass at the center of their daily lives. They must listen and obey Christ's Vicar on earth. They must (as Venerable Fulton Sheen wrote) recognize that their sanctification (as well as ours) starts with a "lively faith in the Divine Presence", "that their holiness makes the Church holy", that their primary concern must "be the tabernacle, not the rectory, not the ego, but the Lord, not [their] comfort, but God's glory", and that "only those who believe the incredible can ever do the impossible".

Our priests certainly would also be well served, as Pope Emeritus Benedict XVI suggested, to reflect on the words spoken to them as newly ordained priests when their Bishop presented them with the chalice and paten: "Understand what you do, imitate what you celebrate, and conform your life to the mystery of the Lord's Cross."

I must hasten to acknowledge that we lay men and women share some blame for the current crisis in the priesthood. We have not fully appreciated our priests, or the enormous demands placed on them, or the unrelenting attack to which the Evil one subjects them. In that sense, we have let these special men down. Too often we have failed to support or encourage them when they have shared the sometimes difficult demands of our Faith. Some of us have actually discouraged them from preaching the Truth.

Whatever we have failed to do, now is the time to make amends. Our priests need us and the power of our prayers. Just as there is no reason for any of them to fear emulating St. John Vianney, there is no Catholic who should hesitate offering a monthly novena to that great saint on behalf of our priests. It is a simple but powerful gift we owe them. You can easily find this novena online. Today would be a great time to begin!

Into The Shelter of My Wounded Side

How it grieves My Heart when the unique love I offer a soul is spurned, or ignored, or regarded with indifference. I tell you this so that you may make reparation to My Heart by accepting the love I have for you and by living in My friendship.

Receive My gifts, My kindnesses, My attention, My mercies for the sake of those who refuse what I so desire to give them. Do this especially for My priests, your brothers. I would fill each one of My priests with My merciful love, I would take each one into the shelter of My wounded Side, I would give to each one the delights of My Divine Friendship, but so few of My priests accept what I desire to give them.

They flee from before My Face. They remain at a distance from My open Heart. They keep themselves apart from Me. Their lives are compartmentalized. They treat with Me only when duty obliges them to do so. There is no gratuitous love, no desire to be with Me for My own sake, simply because I am there in the Sacrament of My Love, waiting for the companionship and friendship of those whom I have chosen and called from among millions of souls to be My priests and to be the special friends of My Sacred Heart.

Would that priests understood that they are called not only to minister to souls in My Name, but even more to cling to Me, to abide in Me, to live in Me and for Me, and by Me and no other. . .

So many of My priests have never really heard and understood the invitation to an exclusive and all-Fulfilling friendship with Me. And so, they feel alone in life. They are driven to seek out in other places and in creatures unworthy of the undivided love of their consecrated hearts, the fullness of happiness, and hope, and peace that only I can give them. So many go forward in bitterness and disappointment. They seek to fill the emptiness within with vain pursuits, with lust, with possessions, with food and drink.

They have Me, very often, near to them in the Sacrament of My Love, and they leave Me there alone, day after day and night after night. Oh, how My Heart longs to raise up a company of priest-adorers who will make reparation for their brother priests by abiding before My Eucharistic Face.

I will pour out the treasures of My Eucharistic Heart upon them. I want to renew the priesthood in My Church, and I will do it beginning with a few priests touched to the quick by My friendship, and drawn into the radiance of My Eucharistic Face. The graces stored up in My Heart for priests are inexhaustible, but so few open themselves to receive them.

(From *In Sinu Iesu*, The Journal of a Priest)

You Pass Me By

[Sometimes, one priest must have the courage to challenge some of his brother priests by writing frankly and truthfully.]

Nothing so grieves my Heart as the coldness and indifference of priests and of consecrated souls to my living presence among them. Had they not the privilege of my abiding Sacramental presence close at hand, they might be excused for the hardness of their hearts, but those who have me near, those who dwell close to my tabernacles have no excuse for the estrangement of their souls from the Sacrament of my Love.

On the Day of Judgment I will hold them accountable for the neglect and indifference by which they alienated themselves from me, while I, the living God, the God who is love, the God who is all mercy and who sought their friendship and their company waited for them, and waited in vain.

Even you, O my priests, my adorers, my chosen friends, consolers of my Heart, disappoint me when, although I wait for you and although it is within your power to approach me, to adore me even for a moment, and to console me, you pass me by and live as though I were not here waiting for you, yearning for your companionship, ready to embrace you.

Come to me, then, come to me as often as you can. Come, even if only for a moment to allow me to refresh you, to inflame you with my love, to illuminate your mind, and to pacify your soul.

Come to me and, for a moment, remain with me for the sake of those who walk away from me. Come to me for the sake of those who pass me by.

Come to me for the sake of those whose hearts are cold and who seek their happiness in passing things. Come to me, and I will welcome you. Come to me, and I will bless you. Come to me, and I will press you against my open Heart. Come to me, and I will show you the beauty of my Eucharistic Face.

Come to me, and your soul shall live. Come to me, and yours shall be the joy that the world cannot give. Come to me, and I will place you next to myself. Come to me, and know that I come to those who come to me, together with my Father and the Holy Spirit.

Come to me, for I wait for you.

(From *In Sinu Iesu*, the Journal of a Priest)

Love's Invisible Radiance

There are so many tabernacles on earth where I am, for all intents and purposes, like one buried, hidden, forgotten, and out of sight. My divine radiance is diminished because there are so few adorers to act as the receptors of My radiant Eucharistic love and to extend My radiance through space and into the universe of souls. Where there is faith in My Real Presence, there will be Adoration; and where there is Adoration, there will also be an efficacious radiance of My Presence drawing souls to My Eucharistic Heart and surrounding them, even at a distance, with the healing influence of My Eucharistic Face.

In those places where I am exposed upon the altar to receive the adoration, the reparation, and the companionship of My friends - and, first of all, of My priests - My radiance is powerful and strong. Faith, adoration, and love act as receptors; thus is My power drawn out and made effective, invisibly but really, in space and in time.

It was the same with My Sacred Humanity during My life on earth; the faith and love of My friends drew out the virtue of My Divinity, and an invisible radiance acted in souls, and upon them, bringing healing, holiness, and many graces of conversion. When I am adored in a place, My hidden action upon souls is wonderfully increased. The place where I am adored becomes a radiant centre from which love, and life, and light are diffused in a world in the grip of hatred, and darkness, and death.

Chapels of adoration are not mere refuges for the devout. They are the radiant, pulsating centres of an intense divine activity that goes beyond the walls of the place where I am adored to penetrate homes, and schools, and hospitals; to reach even those dark and cold places wherein souls are enslaved to Satan; to penetrate hearts, heal the infirm, and call home those who have wandered far from Me. For these reasons, the work of Perpetual Adoration, or even of prolonged daily Adoration, is intensely apostolic and supernaturally efficacious.

Would that My bishops understood this! But, alas, they put their trust in human schemes, in plans devised by the worldly-wise, and in programs drawn-up along shortsighted human principles. And so they go, and they will continue to go from failure to failure, and from disillusionment to disillusionment.

I have not set bishops over My flock to govern, and to teach, and to sanctify, out of their personal abilities and by making use of the wisdom of this passing world. I have set them as lights upon a lamp stand to shine in every dark place, and I have equipped them with supernatural gifts and divine power to accomplish that for which I chose them and set them over My Church.

Woe to those bishops who trust in purely human solutions to the problems that beset My Church. They will be grievously disappointed, and many souls will fall away because they have neglected to take up the supernatural weapons I have prepared for them in this time of spiritual combat.

My Presence in the Blessed Sacrament preached, and confessed, and surrounded by adoration, love, and heartfelt reparation is the single greatest remedy for the evils that afflict My Church and for the sorrows that weigh so heavily upon My priests. My ways are not your ways, nor do I act according to the principles of worldly success. I act in the silent, humble, hidden reality of My Eucharistic Presence. Adore Me, and the radiance of My Eucharistic Face will begin to change the face of the earth, even as it heals My priests, calls sinners home to My Heart, and enlivens the hearts of those grown weary and sad (like the disciples on the road to Emmaus) with a spark of divine vitality and with the fire of My Eucharistic love.

I speak to you in this way not only for you, beloved friend of My Heart, but also for those who will receive these words, ponder them, and out of them draw the inspiration to love Me more generously, more fruitfully, and more joyfully. I speak to you for the sake of My priests. You will be astonished at the reception given to these words of Mine. Many souls of priests will be quickened and consoled by them. Many priests will be moved to spend time in the radiance of My Eucharistic Face, and to abide close to My pierced Heart.

This is My desire for them. I want to draw all My priests into the radiance of My Face and, then, into the sanctuary of My open Heart.

(From *In Sinu Iesu*, The Journal of a Priest)

Every Knee Shall Bend – The Powerful Example of One Holy Priest

A few days ago, I was prompted to read through some older journal entries and discovered one from more than 13 years ago. How timeless are the insights God gives us, especially those we may have forgotten but are blessed to rediscover!

Let me share with you what I wrote (with some editing) more than a decade ago:

"I attended Mass at a Dominican Monastery today. There are no resident Dominican friars there. As I exited my car, I saw an elderly Franciscan priest getting out of his vehicle. He had come to say Mass. He was unable to stand upright. His elderly and frail body was hunched over (literally in half) as he walked carefully on the snow with the aid of a cane, his priestly vestments folded over his other arm.

I asked Father if he needed any help. He joyfully declined my assistance as I held the door leading into the monastery open for him. His walking was deliberate and appeared painful. He was unable to stand erect.

I assumed he would take the elevator, But he surprised me when he laboriously climbed the steps to the second floor chapel. As we approached the chapel door, I opened it for him as well. He entered and fully genuflected before entering the sacristy - his knee touching the floor. It took great effort for him to do that; he was quite unsteady when he got up, still hunched over in half.

I was touched that this priest loved God so much that he ignored his own physical limitations and discomfort in order to provide all of us present with such a visible and powerful sign of his respect, reverence for, and belief in, the Real and Substantial Presence of our Lord, Body, Blood, Soul and Divinity, hidden behind the locked doors of the chapel's tabernacle.

How many of us do not genuflect at all, though fully and physically able to do so?

I was moved throughout the Mass as Father continued to genuflect when required, his knee always touching the floor despite the pain it caused him and the great difficulty he had in getting back up. He was never able to stand upright.

But I was finally brought to tears when Father forced himself by sheer love for the Eucharist and the grace of God to stand fully erect when he lifted Our Lord first in the Sacred and Consecrated Host and then in the Holy Chalice of His Sacred Blood!

What I witnessed and what this priest did was nothing short of miraculous! Despite his physical limitations, He was determined to give honor to the God he so obviously believed was in his hands.

His example should serve as clarion call for the rest of us to always honor our Lord by our words and actions as well."

Thank you God for the holy priests in our midst!

The Holy Sacrifice

of the

Mass

The Greatest Event

That

Could Ever Take Place

on

This Earth

'The Mass is the center and kernel of Catholic worship; without it our faith would die, as it does in those who willfully miss their obligation of attendance at Mass. Those who have so often tried to stamp out the Church have understood this well, for they have always advocated abolishing the Mass. Yet with the Mass we have "the power of God and the wisdom of God" which nothing can restrain. For the Holy Eucharist is not only a sacrament, it is also a sacrifice, the renewal of the Sacrifice of Mount Calvary, whereby the infinite fruits of that sacrifice are applied to our souls."

(Father Desmond Murray, O.P.)

And You Think The Mass Is Boring?

Far too many Catholics complain they find the Mass to be "boring" or that they "get nothing out of it". It is unlikely they would feel that way if they knew the answers to the following questions once posed by Father Peter Girard, O.P.: What is the Holy Sacrifice of the Mass? What happens at Mass? Who is present there? What benefits do we receive by participating at Mass?

In his powerful book, *The Way to God*, Father Winfrid Herbst, S.D.S. tells us that the Holy Sacrifice of the Mass "is not a mere commemoration of the sacrifice of the cross. No it is the same, the actuality, the renewal, the continuation, the representation of the sacrifice of the cross...so that when I assist at Mass I am present at the Sacrifice of the cross as much as Mary, John and Magdalene were. It is the unbloody renewal of the bloody Sacrifice of the cross."

Does this essential truth of our faith come as a surprise to many? How often we Catholics come to Church just to socialize and "catch up" with friends, families and acquaintances. Should we not come primarily to worship, adore, give honor to and receive the King of Kings and Lord of Lords? When we understand what the Mass is, we shall!

When properly understood and when participated in with proper intent, the Holy Sacrifice of the Mass "is offered," as Father Herbst reminds us, "to give God Honor and Glory, to give God thanks for his benefits, to obtain the remission of our sins and make reparation for them, to obtain the precious grace of conversion by which a person is led to make repentance and reconciliation with God, to obtain victory over temptations, either by getting more efficacious actual graces or by having the temptations themselves lessened or eliminated altogether." But there is more, much more to this magnificent gift (see Section 1322-1372 of The Catechism of the Catholic Church).

St. John Marie Vianney taught: "There is nothing so great as the Eucharist. If God had something more precious, He would have given it to us"; and "If we really understood the Mass, we would die of joy". In current times, Father William Casey of the Fathers of Mercy reminds us that "the Holy Sacrifice of the Mass is the most important event that occurs every day on the face of the earth".

"Mass," Pope Pius VI tells us, "is the most powerful form of prayer." "The celebration of Holy Mass," St. Thomas Aquinas writes, "is as valuable as the death of Jesus on the cross." St. Padre Pio also reminded us of four beautiful truths: (1) "It would be easier for the world to survive without the sun than to do so without the Holy Mass;" (2) "The heavens open and multitudes of angels come to assist in the Holy Sacrifice of the Mass;" (3) "If we only knew how God regards this Sacrifice we would risk our lives to be present at a single Mass;" and (4) "The best preparation for a happy death is to assist at Mass daily."

"The Eucharistic Sacrifice, the memorial of the death and resurrection of the Lord, in which the Sacrifice of the cross is forever perpetuated," according to Canon 897, "is the summit and the source of all worship and Christian life." In Canon 898, we are reminded that: "Christ's faithful are to hold the Blessed Eucharist in the highest honor. They should take an active part in the celebration of the most august Sacrifice of the Mass; they should receive the sacrament with great devotion and frequently, and should reverence it with the greatest adoration."

In *The Decree on the Life and Ministry of Priest (Presbyterium Ordinis, note 14)*, the Vatican II fathers observed that the bond which gives unity to the priest's life and work "flows mainly from the Eucharistic Sacrifice, which is therefore the center and root of the whole priestly life". Saint John Paul II noted in his *Encyclical on the Eucharist (Ecclesia de Eucharistia, note 31)*, that the Eucharist "is the source and summit of the Church's life" and that the Holy Sacrifice of the Mass "must be the center of each priest's life". He went on to emphasize that "we must understand then, how important it is, for the spiritual life of the priest as well as for the good of the Church and the world, that priests follow the Council's recommendation to celebrate the Eucharist daily". Short of serious personal illness or an unforeseen and pressing emergency, is there any compelling reason why a priest would not offer Mass each day? After all, who can fathom the benefits flowing from the Holy Sacrifice of the Mass?

Is it any wonder then that both Saint John Paul II and his successor Benedict XVI had repeatedly urged all of us, priest and laity alike, to rediscover a sense of "awe and amazement" in the Eucharist, the Holy Sacrifice of the Mass, and Eucharistic Adoration?

.

I have no doubt we would rediscover that sense of "awe and amazement" for the Holy Sacrifice of the Mass and the Eucharist if, when we next attend, we follow the suggestions offered by Father M. Raymond, O.S.S.O. in his book, *God, A Woman, and The Way*:

> "…when the Host is held on high and a chalice lifted…look up! Look up and see what Mary saw. See a naked man squirming as He bleeds against a blackened sky; see a battered human body, writhing on a tree, prisoned there by savage spikes that have torn through Sacred hands and feet; see thorn-tortured head tossing from side to side as anguished torso labors, lifts and strains; see the eyes of God roll towards heaven beseeching, as broken lips blurt out that soul piercing cry: 'My God, My God, Why has Thou forsaken Me?' What is this? This is the Mass. This is Crucifixion. This is what Mary saw at the elevation of Christianity's first Mass. This is what you should see at the Elevation of every Mass!"

The Wrong Question!

A number of commentators are wringing their hands over what they perceive to be another unfairness that will flow from the revised translations to the Holy Sacrifice of the Mass. How, they lament, will the Catholics who attend Mass only twice a year, be able to participate in a liturgy whose words will be so different from those they last heard?

Wrong question!

The correct one to ask is why are all those Catholics who attend Mass only twice a year not fearful of spending eternity in hell for failing to obey God's commandment? This query should be quickly followed up with two others: Why won't this issue be discussed with these infrequent Mass attendees and why will so few of them be reminded not to approach our Lord in the Holy Eucharist if they have not been fulfilling their obligation to actively participate in weekly Sunday Mass without first bathing themselves in the healing and forgiving waters of a sacramental confession?

In some places (not my parish) fear of offending someone or their feelings will take precedence over concern for the salvation of their souls or the painful and hurtful offense our Lord will be subjected to by those who approach Him in mortal sin. This would never happen if pleasing God was viewed as more important than upsetting man.

There can be nothing more important than saving souls! If one dies in a state of mortal sin, there is no escaping hell. Missing Sunday Mass without a legitimate excuse is a mortal sin, as, for example, are such things as abortion, adultery, contraception, sex outside of marriage, and euthanasia. Yet, there are those professing to be Catholic (recent polls suggesting not few in number) who do not believe this truth. Rarely do they hear anything about hell and mortal sin. Some are simply told of a merciful loving God who gives us "hope that no one is in hell," unambiguous Scriptural references or approved Marian apparitions to the contrary notwithstanding.

Yes, we must warmly welcome all those who come to our Churches each Sunday, and most especially those whom we only see at Christmas and Easter. We must let them know how happy we are to see them, how much God loves them, and how He longs to see them every Sunday. At the same time, our priests cannot let them leave Church without making it certain they understand the eternal consequences if they continue to defy God by skipping Sunday Mass. Sadly, such frankness may have a negative impact on the collections. But this truth can be conveyed lovingly by any priest whose heart is aflame with the passion to save souls. It is an act of charity. It is the duty and obligation of our priests to do so. If not on the only two times each year that so many come to Church, when?

Two examples of priestly zeal for the salvation of souls immediately come to my mind. There are, of course, many others. Saint Dominic established his Order of Preachers "for the salvation of souls through preaching." As Father Garrigou-Lagrange, O.P. has noted, Dominic would "spend practically the whole night in church, praying for and doing penance for the sinners to whom he wanted to preach the Gospel the following day."

Another Dominican, Louis Bertrand, O.P., patron saint of novice masters and mistresses, "cared very little whether he pleased men, but he was very anxious to please God and St. Dominic." He was fond of telling his brothers that "he did not wish to go himself to hell, or even to purgatory on account of the faults of his friends". Less anyone still not understand, he hung a scroll on his cell wall which read: "If I yet pleased men, I should not be the servant of Christ (Gal 1:10)."

All priests must have that same zeal – that is why God called them to the priesthood.

"We owe everyone the Truth," as St. Therese of Lisieux reminds us, "even if that may cause others to dislike us." Our salvation and that of countless others depends on our priests having the courage to teach and speak the Truth.

So let's always ask the right questions.

[We lay people also owe everyone the Truth. We have the same obligation as do our priests to fraternally correct those whose acts or omissions demonstrate they are in jeopardy of losing their souls. Tough to do! Many will not like you for being truthful. They will accuse you of being arrogant, judgmental, and intolerant. Draw comfort and strength knowing that God will be pleased with your efforts and will water the seeds you have planted in the hearts of those you loved enough to share His Truth!]

Are The Masses You Attend Celebrated Worthily and Holily? – Part I

For some time now, I have been reading *The Priest In Union With Christ* written by the late Father Reginald Garrigou-Lagrange, O.P., described by some as "probably the 20th century's greatest theologian" and "one of the Church's all-time greatest authorities on the spiritual life".

Given the on-going attack on the nature of the priesthood, our priests and the Holy Sacrifice of the Mass, this is a book you should read and gift to any priest you treasure.

In it, this gifted Dominican urges all of his readers to always remember "that the principal Priest in the sacrifice of the Mass is Christ, and that the celebrant must be striving for an actual and closer union with Him." Does this truth come as a surprise to you?

He then goes on to describe the different ways of celebrating Mass: the sacrilegious Mass, the Mass which is said hurriedly, the Mass which is outwardly correct but lacks the spirit of faith, the Mass which is faithfully and worthily celebrated, and the Mass of the Saints.

We would all do well to read, reflect and ponder these various descriptions. But I want to focus on the Mass which is faithfully and worthily celebrated – "a Mass offered in a spirit of faith, of confidence in God and of love for God and one's neighbor".

> "In such a sacrifice, we witness the impulse and guidance of the Theological Virtues which inspire the virtue of religion. The *Kyrie Eleison* is a genuine prayer of petition; the *Gloria in Excelsis Deo* is an act of adoration of God on high; the Gospel of the day is read with keen belief in what it contains; the words of Consecration are pronounced by a minister in actual union with Christ the principal Offerer, by one who

66

realizes to some extent the wide diffusion of the spiritual effects of his offering and sacramental immolation to the souls in this world and to those in Purgatory. The *Agnus Dei* is a sincere request for the forgiveness of sin; the priest's Communion leaves nothing to be desired– it is always more fervent and more fruitful than the day before because of the daily growth in charity produced by the Sacrament of the Eucharist. The distribution of Holy Communion is not approached in any perfunctory spirit, but is treated as the means of bestowing on the faithful, superabundant life, of giving them an even greater share in the divine life…Afterwards the priest will make his private thanksgiving, which, if time permits, will be prolonged on certain feast days in the form of mental prayer. There is no more suitable time for intimate prayer than when Christ is Sacramentally present within us, and when our soul, if recollected, is under His actual influence."

But you might be saying that Father Garrigou-Lagrange wrote those words prior to the Mass changes implemented after Vatican II, so they have no relevancy to us today. An expert, I am not, but I do know this: Vatican II never mandated the removal of Latin from the Mass and never, and could never, change its supernatural nature or the reverence with which it must be celebrated. Man did this and we are now paying dearly for those errors.

In my simple layman's mind and with the aid of Father Peter Girard, O.P. and other holy priests, I have come to understand that when we participate in the Holy Sacrifice of the Mass we are really being transported spiritually beyond the realm of earthly time and space and enter into the on-going heavenly liturgy which someday we hope to enjoy. Please correct me if I am in error.

Is this how you experience Mass? How blessed you are!

Are The Masses You Attend Celebrated Worthily and Holily? – Part II

As painful an exercise as the following may be, it would be worthwhile to take a look at two other types of Masses the good Friar (Father Reginald Garrigou-Lagrange, O.P.) describes – "the hurriedly said Mass" and the one that is "outwardly correct but lacks the spirit of faith" - neither of which has resurrected or can resurrect the sense of awe and amazement in the Holy Sacrifice of the Mass and the Eucharist to which Catholics are entitled and that Saint John Paul II advocated and so longed for each of us to experience.

This is, in part, what Father Reginald has to say about a "hurriedly said Mass":

> "This haste in saying Mass shows that the priest has lost sight of the true importance and seriousness of his life. For him it is no longer the Mass that matters most, but outward activity and a pseudo-apostolate. With the disappearance of almost every vestige of an interior life, there has disappeared also every hope of a fruitful apostolate, since that is the heart and soul of any genuine apostolate...
>
> A Mass offered in haste is a scandal, in so far as the Kyrie, Gloria, Credo and Sanctus are recited mechanically, without any spirit of faith...The prayers of the Missal are read as though they were of no importance, whereas they are pregnant with such meaning as will only be fully grasped in the light of the Beatific Vision.
>
> The Mass becomes a mere formula of words, rendering contemplation impossible. And yet,

if there are any words which ought to be recited with the utmost care and contemplative insight, they are the words of the Missal – the Kyrie, the Gloria and the Credo. But in the hasty Mass they are recited mechanically in order to finish Mass more quickly. Genuflections are made with equal haste – empty gestures, devoid of the spirit of worship…"

The wise friar then describes another deficiently celebrated Mass, one that is "outwardly correct but lacks the spirit of faith":

This Mass is one in "which the priest pays careful heed to the external rite, to all the rubrics – perhaps he himself is a keen rubrician - but he offers the Mass as though he were nothing more than a mere ecclesiastical official, seemingly devoid of any spirit of worship. He knows the rubrics and observes them, but he pays little regard to the infinite worth of the Mass or to the principal Offerer whose minister he is. Such a priest is another Christ in outward appearance only, in so far as he possesses the priestly character enabling him to offer Mass validly, but he displays no signs of the true spirit of a priest. It would appear that since the day of his Ordination, Sanctifying Grace and the sacramental grace of Orders have not increased to any appreciable extent, although they were given as a treasure to yield rich dividends.

True the priest who celebrates in this way will think he is saying his Mass extremely well by reason of his scrupulous regard for the rubrics, but that is the limit of his aspirations.

> The Kyrie, Gloria, Credo, Sanctus, the words
> of Consecration and the Communion prayers
> are said without any spirit of belief."

A short handed way to express these concerns is to reference the heading of a column written by Archbishop Charles J. Chaput, O.F.M. Cap. entitled, "How we pray shapes what we believe". The Latin phrase, *lex orandi, lex credendi,* expresses the same concept.

Catholics will unlikely come to a true appreciation and understanding of the Holy Sacrifice of the Mass if all they ever see is a "hurriedly said Mass" or one that is "outwardly correct but lacks the spirit of faith".

The words of Father Garrigou-Lagrange, O.P. are an invitation for all to recognize the Holy Sacrifice of the Mass as the single greatest daily event happening on this planet, and a reminder to all priests, as St. Pius X taught, that "The sanctity of the Christian people depends in large measure on the holiness of their priests."

This great Dominican author and teacher would have appreciated the words of Saint John Paul II: "Liturgy is never anyone's private property, be it of the celebrant or the community in which the mysteries are celebrated...No one is permitted to undervalue the mystery entrusted to our hands; it is too great for anyone to feel free to treat it lightly and with disregard for its sacredness and its universality." (*Ecclesia de Eucharistia, note 52*).

He certainly would have been heartened and encouraged by the expanding availability of the Extraordinary Form of the Holy Sacrifice of the Mass and the recent revisions to the Roman Missal, as should we and our priests.

Pray for our priests, particularly for any who may not treasure the Holy Sacrifice of the Mass as they ought.

I Went to Mass Today. It Was Unlike Most Other Days!

What a privilege it was to serve Mass this morning! It is not something I have had the honor to do more than three or four times in my adult life.

For someone who just recently received his Medicare card, today was both a day for gratitude and for awe – gratitude for the gift of life and awe for the privilege to be so close to the holy altar of sacrifice.

Who am I to have been privileged to unlock Jesus' cell door this morning in anticipation of Father carrying Him out to be with those Whom He so dearly loves?

Or to have prayed with Father in the sacristy before we processed into the sanctuary and after we returned upon the completion of the Holy Sacrifice of the Mass?

How can I ever explain the overwhelming sense of unworthiness and the simultaneous joyful awareness of being so privileged to kneel in the sanctuary just feet from the Last Supper and Calvary, surrounded by our Blessed Mother, St. Joseph, all the saints, the heavenly angels and the souls in purgatory?

Why did God bless me with this privilege on this the feast day of St. Joseph – the namesake of my only son and my deceased father, and the patron Saint of my Dominican province?

What an honor it was to hold a paten under the hands and mouths of those who came to receive the Body, Blood, Soul and Divinity of their Risen Lord and Savior and to return the purified chalice, paten and corporal to its table.

I have known intellectually for some time that the Mass is the greatest event occurring on the face of this earth each day.

Today, I was privileged to intimately live that Truth, up close and personal.

As I put out the candles and retrieved the chalice, paten, corporal and cruets from the table for return to the sacristy, I was prompted to glance over my shoulder. My loving Lord had yet one more gift for me this day.

There, as he frequently does, kneeling in the sanctuary, giving public, powerful but silent witness to his abiding love for the Eucharist, was my pastor – never too busy to spend time with His beloved Lord.

Thank you Lord for the Holy Sacrifice of the Mass! Thank you Lord for Your holy and faithful priests! Thank you for today!

How Great It Was To See You!

I am always here – 24 hours a day, seven days a week, and 365 days a year - waiting for you. But generally I am alone, abandoned and ignored.

So when I looked out from behind the closed doors this morning, I was overjoyed to see you - so many of you. While there were many familiar faces among those filling the pews, there were a good number whom I have not seen in some time. If you only knew the joy I experience when you come!

I take delight in all My people, but I experience a special joy when those who stay away come to be with Me. I have so much to give each of you!

How I hunger for your presence here every Sunday. How I want to be one with you and fill you will My graces. How I want to give you the spiritual nourishment you need to withstand the weekly onslaught and temptations that surround you.

I offer you My Word and most especially My Body, Blood Soul and Divinity!

But if you have not been coming to Sunday Mass, if you have intentionally ignored or disobeyed My commandments, if you have unconfessed mortal sin on your soul, then there is something you must first do before approaching Me at the altar if you are to eternally benefit from Holy Communion.

See that little box, that little room off to the side or in the back of the Church? At least once a week, I sit there in the person of my priest, waiting for you to come, to humble yourself, to acknowledge your sinfulness, to ask for my forgiveness and to resolve to sin no more. My mercy is yours for the asking!

It really isn't that difficult. I already know where you have failed Me, yourself and others. There is nothing You could ever tell my priest that he has not heard or that I have not forgiven through him countless times before. Truth be told, fewer come to see Me in the confessional each week than visit me in my locked tabernacles!

Pride caused your first parents to disobey me and the same pride keeps so many of you away from Me! Swallow your pride! Humble yourself. Come to this place of forgiveness, healing and mercy – the source of new life. I can not shower you with the graces I have for you in Holy Communion unless you do so.

I am sure you can understand then why your absence from Sunday Mass and the confessional saddens Me so! There is rarely any valid reason for you to miss Sunday Mass or for you to approach Me in the Blessed Sacrament unworthily.

I love you! I will always love you!

I can only offer you eternal life. You must choose it!

So please come back to Mass and confession.

I can hardly wait to see you again.

Appendices

Appendix A

Litany of the Most Blessed Sacrament

[I suspect that if this Litany became better known and recited, more of us would rediscover a sense of awe and amazement in, and appreciation for, the magnificent gift of His Real Presence here among us. If you agree, say it regularly and recommend it to others.]

Lord, have mercy. R. Lord, have mercy.
Christ, have mercy. R. Christ, have mercy.
Lord, have mercy. R. Lord, have mercy.

Christ, hear us. R. Christ, graciously hear us.

God the Father of Heaven, R. have mercy on us.
God the Son, Redeemer of the world, R. have mercy on us.
God the Holy Spirit, R. have mercy on us.
Holy Trinity, one God, R. have mercy on us.
Jesus, Eternal High Priest of the Eucharistic Sacrifice, R. have mercy on us.
Jesus, Divine Victim on the Altar for our salvation, R. have mercy on us.
Jesus, hidden under the appearance of bread, R. have mercy on us.
Jesus, dwelling in the tabernacles of the world, R. have mercy on us.

Jesus, really, truly and substantially present in the Blessed Sacrament, R. have mercy on us.

Jesus, abiding in Your fullness, Body, Blood, Soul and
Divinity, R. have mercy on us.
Jesus, Bread of Life, R. have mercy on us.
Jesus, Bread of Angels, R. have mercy on us.
Jesus, with us always until the end of the world, R. have
mercy on us.
Sacred Host, summit and source of all worship and Christian
life, R. have mercy on us.
Sacred Host, sign and cause of the unity of the Church, R.
have mercy on us.
Sacred Host, adored by countless angels, R. have mercy on
us.
Sacred Host, spiritual food, R. have mercy on us.
Sacred Host, Sacrament of love, R. have mercy on us.
Sacred Host, bond of charity, R. have mercy on us.
Sacred Host, greatest aid to holiness, R. have mercy on us.
Sacred Host, gift and glory of the priesthood, R. have mercy
on us.
Sacred Host, in which we partake of Christ, R. have mercy on
us.
Sacred Host, in which the soul is filled with grace, R. have
mercy on us.
Sacred Host, in which we are given a pledge of future glory,
R. have mercy on us.

Blessed be Jesus in the Most Holy Sacrament of the Altar.
Blessed be Jesus in the Most Holy Sacrament of the Altar.
Blessed be Jesus in the Most Holy Sacrament of the Altar.

For those who do not believe in Your Eucharistic presence,
R. have mercy, O Lord.
For those who are indifferent to the Sacrament of Your love,
R. have mercy on us.
For those who have offended You in the Holy Sacrament of
the Altar, R. have mercy on us.

That we may show fitting reverence when entering Your holy temple, R. we beseech You, hear us.
That we may make suitable preparation before approaching the Altar, R. we beseech You, hear us.
That we may receive You frequently in Holy Communion with real devotion and true humility, R. we beseech You, hear us.
That we may never neglect to thank You for so wonderful a blessing, R. we beseech You, hear us.
That we may cherish time spent in silent prayer before You, R. we beseech You, hear us.
That we may grow in knowledge of this Sacrament of sacraments, R. we beseech You, hear us.
That all priests may have a profound love of the Holy Eucharist, R. we beseech You, hear us.
That they may celebrate the Holy Sacrifice of the Mass in accordance with its sublime dignity, R. we beseech You, hear us.
That we may be comforted and sanctified with Holy Viaticum at the hour of our death, R. we beseech You, hear us.
That we may see You one day face to face in Heaven, R. we beseech You, hear us.

Lamb of God, You take away the sins of the world, R. spare us, O Lord.
Lamb of God, You take away the sins of the world, R. graciously hear us, O Lord.
Lamb of God, You take away the sins of the world, R. have mercy on us, O Lord.

V. O Sacrament Most Holy, O Sacrament Divine,
R. all praise and all thanksgiving be every moment Thine.

Let us pray,
Most merciful Father,
You continue to draw us to Yourself
through the Eucharistic Mystery.

Grant us fervent faith in this Sacrament of love,
in which Christ the Lord Himself is contained, offered
and received.

We make this prayer through the same Christ our Lord. R.
Amen.

(Written by St. Peter Julian Eymard, the founder of the Blessed Sacrament Fathers. This litany is
ecclesiastically approved for liturgical use and has the *Nihil Obstat* and *Imprimatur*. *Nihil Obstat*: Very
Reverend Peter J. Kenny, D.D., Diocesan Censor *Imprimatur*: Most Reverend Denis J Hart DD
Titular Bishop of Vagada Vicar General)

(Source: CatholicCulture.org (http://www.catholicculture.org/-.Used with Permission)

Appendix B

Act of Reparation

MY GOD and my Saviour, Jesus, true God and true Man, worthy Victim of the Most High, Living Bread, and Wellspring of Eternal Life: I adore Thee present in the divine Sacrament of the Altar, with all my heart, desiring to make reparation for the indifference, irreverence, and profanations wrought against Thee in this ineffable Mystery.

On Sundays:

PROSTRATE before Thy most holy majesty, I adore Thee for those who are blinded by materialism; for those who will pursue unlawful gain today; for those who will not adore Thee in Thy churches, nor approach Thine altars, nor lift their hearts and minds to Thee on this, the Day of Thy Holy Resurrection.

On Mondays:

PROSTRATE before Thy most holy majesty, I adore Thee for those who would claim mastery over life and death; for those who defraud the worker, oppress the poor, and harden their hearts against strangers; for those who would destroy human life in the sanctuary of the womb; for those who will shed innocent blood today; for those who commit acts of violence and pursue the things that make for war; and for those who would end the life of those whom they judge to be too old, too sick, too frail, or of little value to society.

79

On Tuesdays:

PROSTRATE before Thy most holy majesty, I adore Thee for those who seek Thy Face in obscurity; for those who know not Thy Name, nor Thy Gospel, nor Thy sacrifice of love upon the Cross, nor Thy presence in the Sacrament of Thy Love. I adore Thee for those who seek answers in false teachings; for those who ally themselves with the powers of darkness; and for those who commit blasphemy and sacrilege.

On Wednesdays:

PROSTRATE before Thy most holy majesty, I adore Thee for those who seek love everywhere, save in Thy Heart; for those who, eager for life in abundance, have found only emptiness; for those who, wrapped in the darkness of this world, are blind to Thy light; for those who, suffering, find themselves alone and forsaken; and for those who, deceived by the Evil One, have exchanged the truth for lies.

On Thursdays:

PROSTRATE before Thy most holy majesty, I adore Thee for those whom Thou callest, not servants, but friends: Thine own priests; for those priests who, by their sins, have disfigured thy Face in the eyes of the world and brought shame upon thy Bride, the Church; for those who never tarry in Thy presence; for those who have forgotten the way to Thy tabernacles; for those who have forsaken prayer and for those locked in spiritual combat with the powers of darkness.

On Fridays:

PROSTRATE before Thy most holy majesty, I adore Thee for the children of Israel, who, if they saw revealed the glory that Thou hast veiled in this Most Holy Sacrament would confess Thee, saying: Verily, Thou art a hidden God, the God of Israel, the Saviour.

On Saturdays:

PROSTRATE before Thy most holy majesty, I adore Thee for those who deny, insult, and blaspheme the Immaculate Conception of Thy Mother, Mary most holy, her perpetual Virginity, her sacred name, her privileges, her titles, and her images.

The Act of Reparation concludes:

I ADORE Thee for those who have never adored Thee, and for those who will never know the happiness of praising Thee. Together with my faith, my love, and the offering of myself, I desire to gather up all the love, which Thou didst have in view in creating these souls in Thine own image and likeness to the praise of Thy glory unto the ages of ages. And to sanctify this adoration of mine and make it more pleasing to Thee, O my Saviour, I unite it to the sacrifice of praise offered by Thy Holy Catholic Church, from the rising of the sun even to the going down of the same.

LOOK Thou to my intentions more than to my words: I desire to utter all that the Holy Spirit has ever inspired Thy Most Holy Mother and Thy Saints to say to Thee; all that Thou sayest to Thy Father in this Sacrament, where Thou offerest Thyself to Him in a perpetual holocaust; and all that Thou sayest to Him in the silence of His bosom where Thou art begotten from all eternity, consubstantial with the Father and with the Holy Spirit, one God forever and ever. Amen.

Appendix C

Litany of Reparation

Lord, have mercy on us.
Lord, have mercy on us

Christ, have mercy on us.
Christ, have mercy on us.

Lord, have mercy on us.
Lord, have mercy on us.

Christ, hear us.
Christ, hear us.

Christ, graciously hear us.
Christ, graciously hear us.

God the Father of Heaven,
Have mercy on us.
God the Son, Redeemer of the world,
Have mercy on us.
God the Holy Spirit,
Have mercy on us.
Holy Trinity, One God,
Have mercy on us.
Sacred Host, offered for the salvation of sinners,
Have mercy on us.
Sacred Host, annihilated on the altar for us and by us,
Have mercy on us.
Sacred Host, despised by lukewarm Christians,
Have mercy on us.
Sacred Host, mark of contradiction,
Have mercy on us.
Sacred Host, delivered over to unbelievers and heretics,
Have mercy on us.

Sacred Host, insulted by blasphemers,
Have mercy on us.
Sacred Host, Bread of angels, given to animals,
Have mercy on us.
Sacred Host, flung into the mud and trampled underfoot,
Have mercy on us.
Sacred Host, dishonored by unfaithful priests,
Have mercy on us.
Sacred Host, forgotten and abandoned in Thy churches,
Have mercy on us.

Be merciful unto us,
Pardon us, O Lord.
Be merciful unto us,
Hear us, O Lord.

For the outrageous contempt of this most wonderful
Sacrament,
We offer Thee our reparation.
For Thine extreme humiliation in Thine admirable
Sacrament,
We offer Thee our reparation.
For all unworthy Communions,
We offer Thee our reparation.
For the irreverences of wicked Christians,
We offer Thee our reparation.
For the profanation of Thy sanctuaries,
We offer Thee our reparation.
For the holy ciboriums dishonored and carried away by force,
We offer Thee our reparation.
For the continual blasphemies of impious men,
We offer Thee our reparation.
For the obduracy and treachery of heretics,
We offer Thee our reparation.
For the unworthy conversations carried on in Thy holy
temples,
We offer Thee our reparation.

For the profaners of Thy churches
which they have desecrated by their sacrileges,
We offer Thee our reparation.

That it may please Thee to increase in all Christians
the reverence due to this adorable Mystery,
we beseech Thee, hear us.
That it may please Thee to manifest the Sacrament
of Thy Love to heretics,
we beseech Thee, hear us.
That it may please Thee to grant us
the grace to atone for their hatred
by our burning love for Thee,
we beseech Thee, hear us.
That it may please Thee
that the insults of those who outrage Thee
may rather be directed against ourselves,
we beseech Thee, hear us.
That it may please Thee graciously
to receive this our humble reparation,
we beseech Thee, hear us.
That it may please Thee to make our adoration acceptable to
Thee,
we beseech Thee, hear us.

Pure Host,
hear our prayer.
Holy Host,
hear our prayer.
Immaculate Host,
hear our prayer.
Lamb of God, Who takest away the sins of the world,
Spare us, O Lord.
Lamb of God, Who takest away the sins of the world,
Graciously hear us, O Lord.
Lamb of God, Who takest away the sins of the world,
Have mercy on us.
V. See, O Lord, our affliction,
R. *And give glory to Thy Holy Name.*

I Thirst For Your Love

Let us pray.
O Lord Jesus Christ,
Who dost deign to remain with us
in Thy wonderful Sacrament unto the end of the world,
in order to give eternal glory to Thy Father,
by the perpetual oblation of Thy Passion,
and to give to us the Bread of life everlasting:
Grant us, we beseech Thee, the grace to mourn,
with a heart full of sorrow,
over the injuries which Thou hast received
in this adorable Mystery,
and over the many sacrileges
which are committed by the impious and by heretics,
and even alas, by weak, ignorant, and wicked Catholics.
Inflame us with an ardent zeal
to repair all the ignominies to which,
in Thine infinite mercy,
Thou hast preferred to expose Thyself
rather than deprive us of Thy Presence on our altars,
Who with God the Father
and the Holy Spirit
livest and reignest one God, world without end. Amen

About The Author

Michael Seagriff practiced law for 30 years, as a general practitioner, prosecutor, criminal defense attorney and Administrative Law Judge.

His vocation as a Lay Dominican created an insatiable desire to learn, study, live and share his Faith. For more than ten years he led a Prison Ministry program and has spent more then twelve years promoting Perpetual Eucharistic Adoration, serving as coordinator of that devotion in his former parish. He always wanted to write and share these experiences but never seemed to have the time when he was working. All that changed unexpectedly in 2009 when he retired.

His written articles have been published in *Homiletic & Pastoral Review*, *The Catholic Sun*, a weekly diocesan newspaper, on *Catholic Exchange.com CatholicLane.com*, *CatholicOnline*, *Catholic Writers Guild Blog*, and *Zenit.org*.

This Lay Dominican has authored three other books: *Forgotten Truths To Set Faith Afire! – Words to Challenge, Inspire and Instruct*, *Fleeting Glimpses of the Silly, Sentimental and Sublime*, and *Pondering Tidbits of Truth*.

Seagriff acquired his healthy sense of humor and his love for the Catholic Faith from his deceased Dad and Mom and employs both frequently, sometimes to the joy and at other times to the consternation of those closest to him.

When not writing, pursing a newly discovered interest in photography, or spending time before the Blessed Sacrament, he enjoys experiencing the pleasures of this earthly life with his loving wife Lonnie, their three children, their spouses and four grandchildren.
He blogs at:
http://harvestingthefruitsofcontemplation.blogspot.com/.

Other Books By Author

Forgotten Truths to Set Faith Afire! – Words To Challenge, Inspire and Instruct - Want to know more about the Catholic faith but don't think you have the time? I have done the heavy lifting for you by compiling more than 1200 quotations from Sacred Scripture, the Catechism of the Catholic Church, Popes, Church Doctors, saints, bishops, priests, sinners and regular folk.

These essential but often *Forgotten Truths* opened the author's eyes, spoke to his heart, and stirred his soul. The power of these words changed his life and can do the same for all who read and reflect upon them.

Fleeting Glimpses of the Silly, Sentimental and Sublime – The author hopes that something you read in this book's twenty essays and personal reflections might bring you laughter at a time you feel forlorn, comfort when you are overburdened with the challenges of daily living, tears of joy when certain words you read or images they generate resurrect thoughts of those you loved and lost, greater appreciation for the gift of life, zeal for the salvation of your soul, and an increased desire to give to God and those He created what He and they deserve.

Pondering Tidbits of Truth - This book recognizes two realities of contemporary life: we are all busy people and many of us have convinced ourselves that we simply do not have the time to read, ponder and reflect on the wealth of spiritual wisdom our Catholic Church has accumulated over the centuries. Yet, we owe God and ourselves this reflective time.

If we spend little or no time pondering the truths and mysteries of our Faith, we are not going to progress spiritually

- a growth essential to our eternal well-being and that of those around us.

Among the 100 quotations in this book, some may be familiar to you - others maybe not so much. All of them offer much fruit for your reflection and contemplation.

All of the author's books are available at Amazon.com.

Made in the USA
Middletown, DE
21 June 2015